Reader's Digest Kids™

Published by The Reader's Digest Association, Inc.

Created and produced by David Bennett Books Limited

This compilation and foreword copyright © 1992 Beverly Mathias
Illustrations copyright © 1992 Alan Snow

Library of Congress Cataloging in Publication Data

Reader's Digest children's book of poetry / selected by Beverly
    Mathias: illustrated by Alan Snow.
        p.   cm.
    Includes index.
    Summary: A collection of poems by such authors as Lois Lenski,
Myra Cohn Livingston, and Aileen Fisher.
    ISBN 0-89577-442-9
    1. Children's poetry, American.   [1. American poetry—
Collections.]   I. Mathias, Beverly.   II. Snow, Alan, ill.
III. Reader's Digest Association.   IV. Title: Children's book of
poetry.
PS586.3.R44   1992
811.008′09282—dc20   92-14698
                                      CIP
                                      AC

Printed in Singapore

Reader's Digest Fund for the Blind is publisher of the Large-Type Edition of *Reader's Digest*. For subscription information about this magazine, please contact Reader's Digest Fund for the Blind, Inc., Dept. 250, Pleasantville, N.Y. 10570.

Reader's Digest
Children's Book of
POETRY

Selected by Beverley Mathias • Illustrated by Alan Snow

READER'S DIGEST KIDS

Pleasantville, N.Y.—Montreal

Introduction

Poetry is an excellent and enjoyable way of expanding a child's language, for it reveals different ways of saying things, links words in strange orders, experiments with images and sounds, and offers the child a myriad of opportunities to see how language works. Young children love the sound of language; they experiment with it, rolling it around, playing with it and enjoying it. The poetry in this collection has been chosen specifically to share with children past the stage of nursery rhymes, for those two or three years prior to starting school. Reading these poems aloud with a child gives you the chance to discuss words and language, and to share noisy times, as well as quieter moments. Some of these poems contain images; some tell stories. Some of them are for thinking about; others are simply for the sheer joy and exuberance of the words.

Beverly Mathias.

Contents

Sing a song of people

Sing a song of people
    Walking fast or slow;
People in the city,
    Up and down they go.

People on the sidewalk,
People on the bus;
People passing, passing,
In back and front of us.
People on the subway
Underneath the ground;
People riding taxis
Round and round and round.

People walking singly,
People in a crowd;
People saying nothing,
People talking loud.
People laughing, smiling,
Grumpy people too;
People who just hurry
And never look at you!

Sing a song of people
Who like to come and go;
Sing of city people
You see but never know!

Lois Lenski

Brother

I had a little brother
And I brought him to my mother
And I said I want another
Little brother for a change.
But she said don't be a bother
So I took him to my father
And I said this little bother
Of a brother's very strange.

But he said one little brother
Is exactly like another
And every little brother
Misbehaves a bit he said.
So I took the little bother
From my mother and my father
And I put the little bother
Of a brother back to bed.

Mary Ann Hoberman

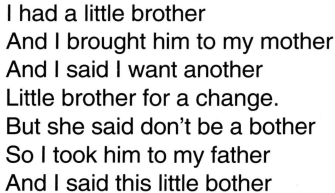

My sister Laura

My sister Laura's bigger than me
And lifts me up quite easily.
I can't lift her, I've tried and tried:
She must have something heavy inside.

Spike Milligan

When I was three

When I was three I had a friend
Who asked me why bananas bend,
I told him why, but now I'm four,
I'm not so sure . . .

Richard Edwards

In the cupboard

I went to the cupboard
And what did I see?
    One lemon
    Two oranges
    Three apples
    Four pears
    Five peaches
    Six plums
    Seven bananas
    Eight cherries
    Nine gooseberries
    Ten raspberries
And up on the shelf
All by itself –
A BIRTHDAY CAKE FOR ME!

Barbara Ireson

Monday's child

Monday's child is fair of face,

Tuesday's child is full of grace,

Wednesday's child is full of woe,

Thursday's child has far to go,

Friday's child is loving and giving,

Saturday's child works hard for its living,

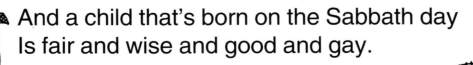

And a child that's born on the Sabbath day
Is fair and wise and good and gay.

Procession

Here comes the bridegroom
Bride upon his arm,
Here comes the best man
Putting on the charm,
Winking at the bridesmaids
Dressed up very fine,
And trying to stop the little ones
From getting out of line;
Here come the mothers
In their fancy hats,
Walking with the fathers,
Having little chats,

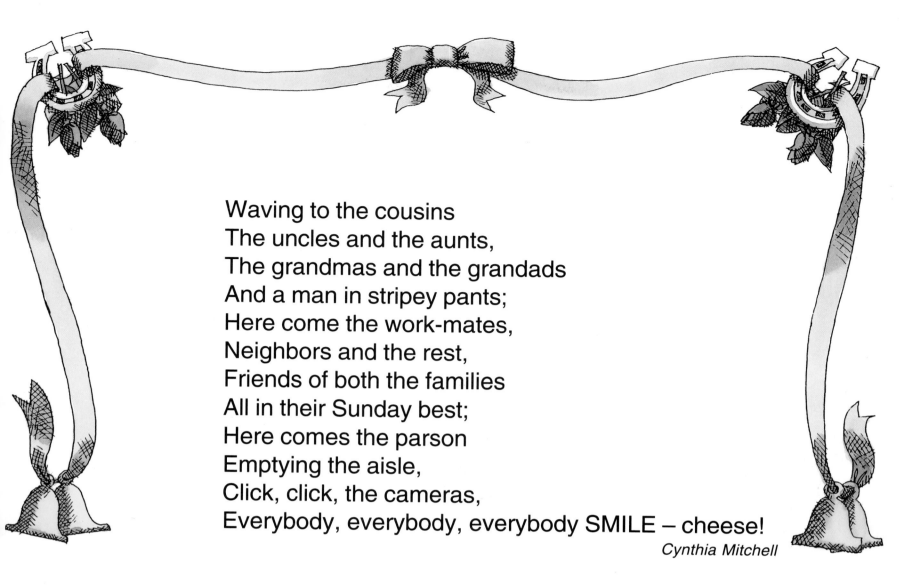

Waving to the cousins
The uncles and the aunts,
The grandmas and the grandads
And a man in stripey pants;
Here come the work-mates,
Neighbors and the rest,
Friends of both the families
All in their Sunday best;
Here comes the parson
Emptying the aisle,
Click, click, the cameras,
Everybody, everybody, everybody SMILE – cheese!

Cynthia Mitchell

Tumbling

In jumping and tumbling
    We spend the whole day,
Till night by arriving
    Has finished our play.

What then? One and all,
    There's no more to be said,
As we tumbled all day,
    So we tumble to bed.

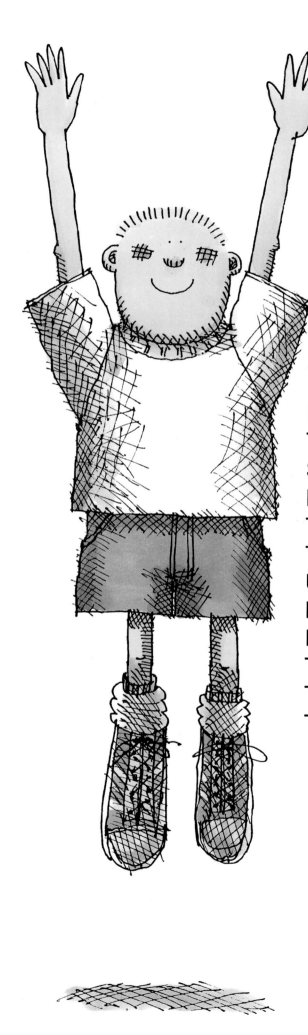

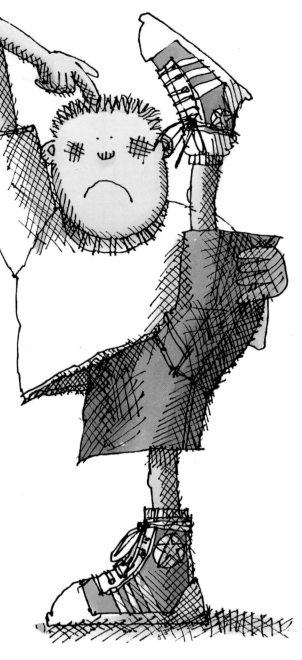

Hands up

Reach for the ceiling
Touch the floor,
Stand up again,
Let's do more.
Touch your head,
Then your knee;
Up to your shoulder,
Like this, see.
Reach for the ceiling
Touch the floor.
That's all now –
There is no more.

17

Rain

Summer rain
    is soft and cool,
    so I go barefoot
    in a pool.

But winter rain
    is cold, and pours,
    so I must watch it
    from indoors.
Myra Cohn Livingston

The rain

Rain on the green grass,
    And rain on the tree,
And rain on the housetop,
    But not upon me!

Get wet? Who? Me?

When I go walking in the rain
I wear a plastic coat,
And rain boots that go slosh, slosh, slosh
Through puddles on the road.

I take my red umbrella, or
Put on a plastic hat;
How could I *possibly* get wet
When I'm dressed like that?

Eva May and Lindy-Ann Moore

The wind

What can be the matter
    With Mr. Wind today?
He calls for me so loudly,
    Through the key-hole, "Come and play."

I'll put my warm red jacket on
    And pull my hat on tight,
He'll never get it off, although
    He tries with all his might.

I'll stand so firm upon my legs,
    I'm strong, what do I care?
Now, Mr. Wind, just come along
    And blow me if you dare.

Dorothy Gradon

A song of the wind

Hark to the song of the scattering, scurrying,
Blustering, bullying, bellowing, hurrying Wind!
Over the hills it comes, laughing and rollicking,
Curling and whirling, flying and frolicking,
Spinning the clouds that are scattered and thinned.
    And shouting a song
    As it gallops along –
A song that is nothing but wind.

This is the song of the galloping, hurrying,
Gusty, and dusty, and whirling, and worrying Wind.
Over the hills it comes, laughing and rollicking,
Yelling and swooping, and flying, and frolicking,
Shaking the fences so solidly pinned,
    And shrieking a song
    As it gallops along –
A terrible song that is Wind.

Will Lawson

Four seasons

Spring is showery, flowery, bowery.
Summer: hoppy, choppy, poppy.
Autumn: wheezy, sneezy, freezy.
Winter: slippy, drippy, nippy.

Weather

Whether the weather be fine,
Or whether the weather be not,
Whether the weather be cold,
Or whether the weather be hot,
We'll weather the weather
Whatever the weather,
Whether we like it or not!

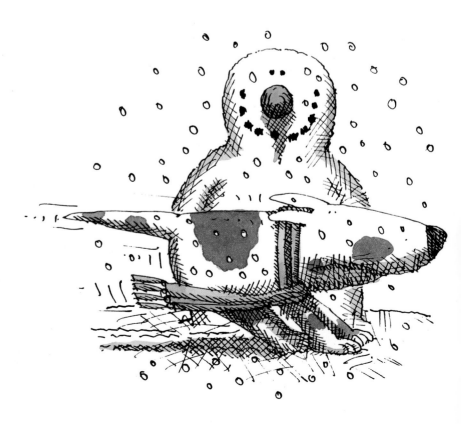

The sun

Every day coming,
every day going,
bringing a goldness
out of the black,

Every day climbing
over the heavens,
sinking at sunset,
soon to be back,

Coming and going,
going and coming,
leaving no footprint,
leaving no track.

Aileen Fisher

The farmyard

One black horse standing by the gate,
Two plump cats eating from a plate;
Three big goats kicking up their heels,
Four pink pigs full of grunts and squeals;
Five white cows coming slowly home,

Six small chicks, starting off to roam;
Seven fine doves perched upon the shed,
Eight gray geese eager to be fed;
Nine young lambs full of frisky fun,
Ten brown bees buzzing in the sun.

A A Attwood

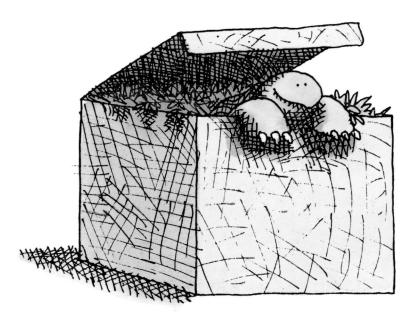

The little turtle

There was a little turtle.
He lived in a box.
He swam in a puddle.
He climbed on the rocks.

He snapped at a mosquito.
He snapped at a flea.
He snapped at a minnow.
And he snapped at me.

He caught the mosquito.
He caught the flea.
He caught the minnow.
But he didn't catch me.

Vachel Lindsay

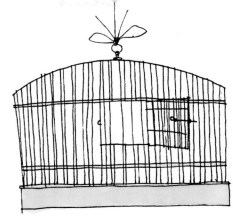

Pussycat, pussycat

Pussycat, pussycat, where have you been,
Licking your lips with your whiskers so clean?
Pussycat, pussycat, purring and pudgy,
Pussycat, pussycat. WHERE IS OUR BUDGIE?

Max Fatchen

If you should meet a crocodile...

If you should meet a crocodile,
        Don't take a stick and poke him;
Ignore the welcome in his smile,
        Be careful not to stroke him.
For as he sleeps upon the Nile,
        He thinner gets and thinner;
And whene'er you meet a crocodile
        He's ready for his dinner.

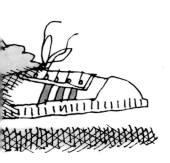

A zoo party

I'd like to give a party
And ask them all to tea:
The alligator, antelope,
The owl and chimpanzee;
The elephant and eagle;
The fox and the gazelle;
The tiger and the llama;
The octopus and snail;
The python and the pelican.
I'd ask them all to come,
And, of course, I'd have the penguins
Or it wouldn't be such fun.

I'd have the lion cubs for sure.
I must have polar bears.
I'd like to have a walrus,
And the wild cat - if she cares;
I'd have - but, when I think of it,
What would we have to eat?
And I wouldn't like the tiger
To come and share *my* seat.
It scarcely would be pleasant,
To say the very least,
To give the Zoo a party
And find *I* was the feast.

Alexander Reid

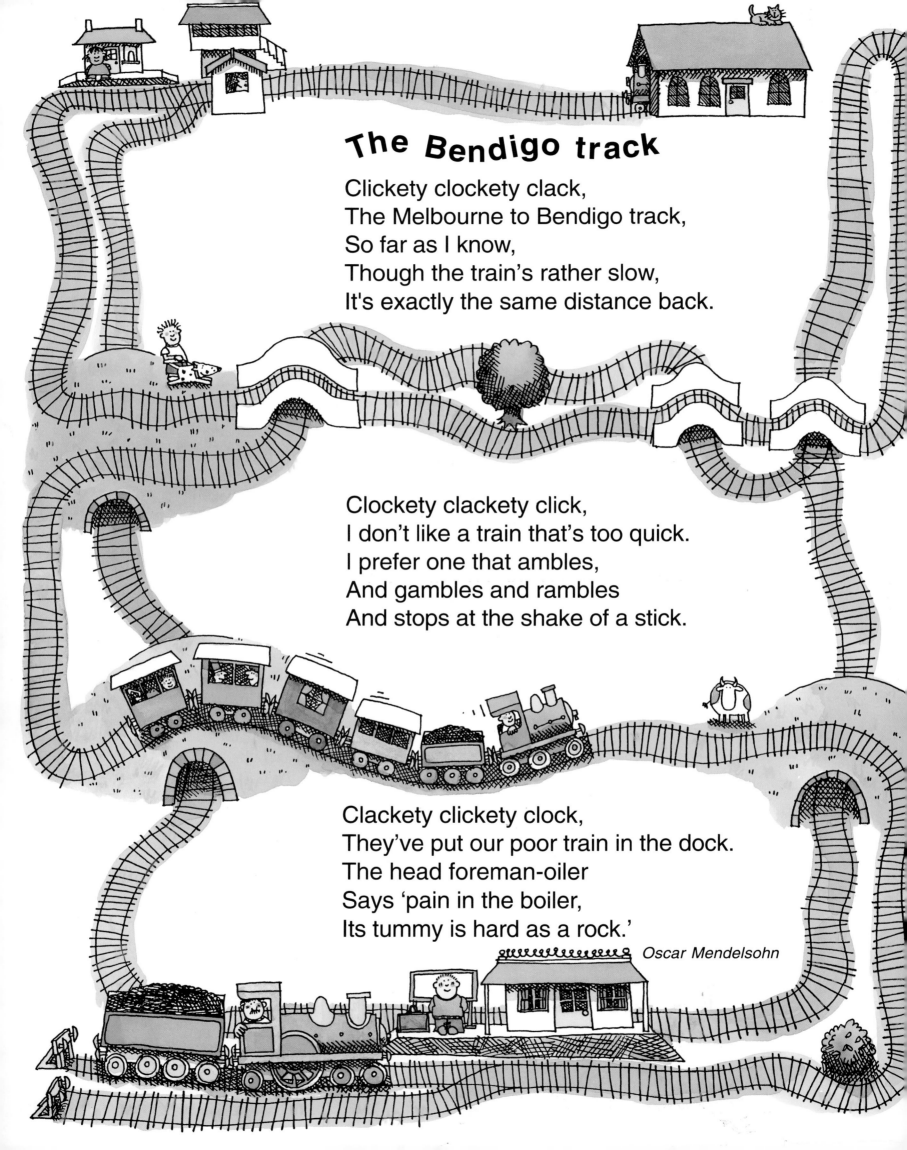

The Bendigo track

Clickety clockety clack,
The Melbourne to Bendigo track,
So far as I know,
Though the train's rather slow,
It's exactly the same distance back.

Clockety clackety click,
I don't like a train that's too quick.
I prefer one that ambles,
And gambles and rambles
And stops at the shake of a stick.

Clackety clickety clock,
They've put our poor train in the dock.
The head foreman-oiler
Says 'pain in the boiler,
Its tummy is hard as a rock.'

Oscar Mendelsohn

Engineers

Pistons, valves and wheels and gears
That's the life of engineers
Thumping, chunking engines going
Hissing steam and whistles blowing.

There's not a place I'd rather be
Than working round machinery
Listening to that clanking sound
Watching all the wheels go round.

Jimmy Garthwaite

31

The balloon

I went to the park
And I bought a balloon.
It sailed through the sky
Like a large orange moon.
It bumped and it fluttered
And swam with the clouds.
Small birds flew around it
In high chirping crowds.
It bounced and it balanced
And bowed with the breeze.
It skimmed past the leaves
On the tops of the trees.
And then as the day
Started turning to night
I gave a short jump
And I held the string tight
And home we all sailed
Through the darkening sky,
The orange balloon, the small birds
And I.

Karla Kuskin

A kite

I often sit and wish that I
Could be a kite up in the sky,
And ride upon the breeze and go
Whichever way I chanced to blow.

Echo

Hello!
  hello!
Are you near?
  near, near.
Or far from here?
  far, far from here.
Are you there?
  there, there
Or coming this way,
Haunting my words
Whatever I say?

Halloo!
  halloooo
Listen, you.
Who are you, anyway?
  who, who, whoooo?

Sara Asheron

I speak, I say, I talk

Cats purr.
Lions roar.
Owls hoot.
Bears snore.
Crickets creak.
Mice squeak.
Sheep baa.
But I SPEAK!

34

Monkeys chatter.
Cows moo.
Ducks quack.
Doves coo.
Pigs squeal.
Horses neigh.
Chickens cluck.
But I SAY!

Flies hum.
Dogs growl.
Bats screech.
Coyotes howl.
Frogs croak.
Parrots squawk.
Bees buzz.
But I TALK!

Arnold L Shapiro

Shoes have tongues

Shoes have tongues,
But cannot talk;
Tables have legs,
But cannot walk;

Needles have eyes,
But cannot see;
Chairs have arms,
But they can't hug me!

Ilo Orleans

I can...

I can tie my shoe lace,
I can brush my hair,
I can wash my hands and face
And dry myself with care.

I can clean my teeth too,
And fasten up my frocks.
I can say 'How do you do'
And pull up both my socks.

A centipede

A centipede was happy quite,
    Until a frog in fun
Said, "Pray, which leg comes after which?"
This raised her mind to such a pitch,
She lay distracted in the ditch
    Considering how to run.

After a bath

After my bath
I try, try, try
to wipe myself
till I'm dry, dry, dry.

Hands to wipe
and fingers and toes
and two wet legs
and a shiny nose.

Just think how much
less time I'd take
if I were a dog
and could shake, shake, shake.

Aileen Fisher

Splash

Nanny baths me all the week,
Tuesday, Wednesday, Monday:
Daddy baths me now and then,
Mommy's day is Sunday.

Nanny is good at it;
Mommy is better;
Nanny's <u>quite</u> good at it . . .
But Daddy is WETTER!

Irene and Aubrey de Selincourt

Six o'clock and after

Six o'clock is bath-time,
Splashing time and fun,
Warm time, cosy time,
When other games are done.

Seven o'clock is bed-time,
Up the stairs I ride,
High on Daddy's shoulder,
With Mommy at our side.

Bed-time is candle-time,
Loveliest light to see,
Best time for stories and
Daddy and me.

Irene and Aubrey de Selincourt

Sailing to sea

I'm sailing to sea in the bathroom,
    And I'm swimming to sea in a tub,
And the only song that I ever will sing
    Is rub-a-dub rub-a-dub dub.

A duck and a dog and a submarine
    Are sailing together with me,
And it's rub-a-dub dub
And it's rub-a-dub dub
    As we all sail out to sea.

Dennis Lee

39

Tree house

A tree house, a free house,
A secret you and me house,
A high up in the leafy branches
Cozy as can be house.

A street house, a neat house,
Be sure and wipe your feet house
Is not my kind of house at all –
Let's go and live in a tree house.

Shel Silverstein

The very nicest place

The fish lives in the brook,
The bird lives in the tree,
But home's the very nicest place
For someone small like me.

Countdown

There are ten ghosts in the pantry,
There are nine upon the stairs,
There are eight ghosts in the attic,
There are seven on the chairs,
There are six within the kitchen,

There are five along the hall,
There are four upon the ceiling,
There are three upon the wall,
There are two ghosts on the carpet,
Doing things that ghosts will do,
There is one ghost right behind me
Who is oh so quiet . . . BOO.

Jack Prelutsky

Acknowledgements

The compiler and publishers would like to thank the following for their kind permission to include copyright material:

Sara Asheron: *'Echo'* by Sara Asheron appeared originally in 'Catch Your Breath', a Lilian Moore collection. Copyright © 1973 by Sara Asheron.

Richard Edwards: *'When I was three'* from 'The Word Party', Lutterworth 1986, reprinted by permission of John Johnson Ltd.

Max Fatchen: *'Pussycat, pussycat'* reprinted by kind permission of John Johnson Ltd, and Penguin Books Ltd, from 'Wry Rhymes for Troublesome Times' by Max Fatchen, (Kestrel Books 1983), copyright © Max Fatchen 1983.

Aileen Fisher: *'After a bath'* and *'The sun'* reprinted by kind permission of the author.

Jimmy Garthwaite: *'Engineers'* from 'Puddin' An' Pie' by Jimmy Garthwaite, copyright 1929 by HarperCollins Publishers, renewed © 1957 by Mirle Garthwaite. Reprinted by permission of HarperCollins Publishers.

Dorothy Gradon: *'The wind'* taken from 'The Book of a Thousand Poems', compiled by J Murray Macbain, reproduced by permission of Unwin Hyman Ltd. © Evans Bros.

Mary Ann Hoberman: *'Brother'* reprinted by permission of Gina Maccoby Literary Agency. Copyright © 1959, renewed 1987 by Mary Ann Hoberman.

Barbara Ireson: *'In the cupboard'* reprinted by permission of the author from 'Over and Over Again' by Barbara Ireson and Christopher Rowe, published by Hutchinson Children's Books.

Karla Kuskin: *'The balloon'* from 'In the Middle of the Trees' copyright © 1986 by Karla Kuskin. Reprinted by permission of the author.

Dennis Lee: *'Sailing to sea'* by Dennis Lee from 'Jelly Belly', published by Macmillan of Canada, © Dennis Lee.

Vachel Lindsay: *'The Little Turtle'* reprinted with permission of Macmillan Publishing Company from 'Collected Poems of Vachel Lindsay'. Copyright 1920 by Macmillan Publishing Company, renewed 1948 by Elizabeth C. Lindsay.

Myra Cohn Livingston: *'Rain'* from 'Whispers and other poems' by Myra Cohn Livingston, © 1958 by Myra Cohn Livingston, reprinted by permission of Marian Reiner for the author.

Oscar Mendelsohn: *'The Bendigo track'* reprinted by permission of Edna Mendelsohn.

Spike Milligan: *My sister Laura'* reprinted by permission of Spike Milligan Productions Ltd.

Eva May and Lindy Ann Moore: *'Get Wet? Who? Me?'* from 'Of This And That' written by Eva May and illustrated by Lindy Ann Moore, reprinted by permission of Eva May.

Jack Prelutsky: *'Countdown'* from 'It's Hallowe'en' by Jack Prelutsky, copyright © 1977 by Jack Prelutsky, reprinted by permission of Greenwillow Books, a division of William Morrow and Co., Inc..

Alexander Reid: *'A zoo party'* reprinted by permission of David Higham Associates Ltd, from 'Zoological Rhymes' by Alexander Reid, published by The Bodley Head.

Irene and Aubrey de Selincourt: *'Six O'Clock and After'* and *'Splash'*, from 'Six O'Clock and After' by Irene and Aubrey de Selincourt, published by Random Century.

Arnold Shapiro: *'I Speak, I Say, I Talk'* from 'Once Upon a Time', Volume 1 of 'Childcraft—The How and Why Library' © 1991 World Book, Inc. By permission of the publisher.

Shel Silverstein: *'Tree house'* from 'Where The Sidewalk Ends' written and illustrated by Shel Silverstein. Copyright © 1974 by Evil Eye Music, Inc.

While every effort has been made to secure permission, we may have failed in a few cases to trace the copyright holder. We apologise for any apparent negligence.

Index of first lines and authors